What Kind of Animal?

Orlando Austin New York San Diego Toronto London

Visit *The Learning Site!*
www.harcourtschool.com

Animals with a Backbone

How many animals can you name? Lizards, hamsters, dogs, and giraffes are all animals. Parrots and monkeys are animals, too. These animals don't look alike at all. But they all have one thing in common. They all have a backbone. That makes each of these animals a vertebrate. **Vertebrates** have a backbone.

Animals with a backbone usually have large brains. They have good vision and hearing. They have strong senses of smell, touch, and taste. These traits help them survive.

All cats, big and small, are vertebrates.

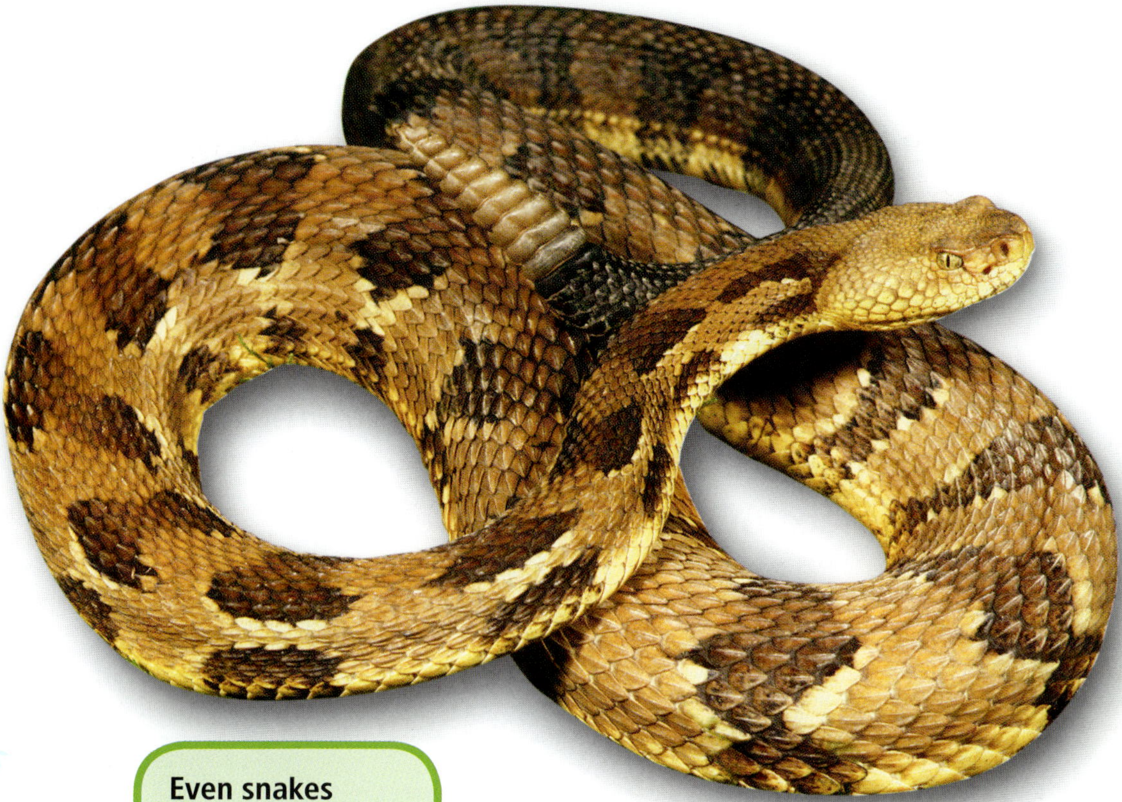

Even snakes are vertebrates because they have a backbone.

There are a lot of vertebrates. Scientists divide vertebrates into five groups. The vertebrates are put into groups based on their traits. Each group is different from each other group. Yet they all have a backbone.

Guess what other animal is a vertebrate? You are! You can feel your backbone when you bend over.

MAIN IDEA AND DETAILS **What do all vertebrates have in common?**

Marvelous Mammals

There are five different groups of vertebrates. One group is mammals. **Mammals** have hair or fur. Fur and hair can help mammals stay warm.

Mammals also have lungs. They take in oxygen from the air using these lungs. Some mammals live underwater. They are called marine mammals. Whales are marine mammals. They need to come to the surface of the ocean to breathe.

See that water flying? The whale is letting its breath out. It blows the water away!

Most mammals give live birth. You are a mammal. If you have any brothers or sisters, you know that they did not hatch from an egg.

Milk made by the mammal mother's body is given to feed young mammals. Most mammals are covered with hair or fur. They can also use their lungs to breathe air.

Fast Fact

Some mammals like to keep their young close by. Koalas have a pouch. When a young koala is born, the mother keeps it in her pouch until it gets bigger.

MAIN IDEA AND DETAILS **Name at least one trait that every mammal shares.**

Most mammals care for their young.

Beautiful Birds

You probably already know what a bird looks like. A **bird** is a vertebrate that has feathers. Like mammals, birds have backbones and lungs. However, birds are different than mammals in several ways. Birds have feathers instead of hair or fur. They have wings and beaks. They lay eggs.

Birds often lay their eggs in nests. One bird will usually sit on top of the eggs to keep them warm until they hatch. Inside each egg is a young bird. Female birds do not make milk to feed their young. Birds must bring food to their young.

Puffins never leave the nest alone. While one parent is hunting, the other is guarding the eggs.

Feathers help birds. Birds fluff out their feathers to stay warm. Feathers cover each bird's wings. Their feathers and wings allow most birds to fly. Birds have hollow bones, so they don't weigh much. Being light makes it easier for them to fly.

Birds use their beaks to get and eat food. Some birds have straight beaks, good for eating seeds. Chickens have straight beaks. Other birds have curved sharp beaks and claws. They use their claws to catch other animals for food.

COMPARE AND CONTRAST **How are birds different from mammals?**

This Philippine eagle is a fierce hunter. He can grow up to 3 feet tall!

Really Cool Reptiles

Reptiles are another group of vertebrates. They all have a backbone. Like mammals and birds, they breathe with lungs. However, they do not have either fur or feathers. Instead, they have dry skin that is covered with scales.

Snakes are reptiles. Many people think that snakes are slimy. If you have ever touched a snake, you know that they are not. They feel dry. Like birds, most reptiles lay eggs. A cobra, for example, may lay 30 eggs at once. When the eggs hatch, the young are on their own.

Snakes don't have arms or legs, but they can still hunt.

Sea turtles lay many eggs on beaches. When they hatch, the young rush into the sea!

Lizards are reptiles, too. They have skin covered with layers of tiny scales. They also lay eggs.

Some reptiles can spend time on land or under water. Sea turtles, crocodiles, and alligators can swim in the sea or walk on land. They have webbed feet, or skin between their toes, to help them swim better. Still, they all need to come to the surface to breathe.

Fast Fact

Reptiles have been around for quite a while. Scientists believe that some dinosaurs were reptiles. Many laid eggs and had dry skin covered with scales!

COMPARE AND CONTRAST **How are reptiles, birds, and mammals similar?**

Amazing Amphibians

You may change as you get older. Still, you don't change as much as an amphibian! **Amphibians** are a group of vertebrates. They spend part of their lives in water and part on land. They change a lot as they grow and get ready to live on land. Unlike reptiles, amphibians have moist skin and lay their eggs in the water.

Frogs are amphibians. Young frogs are called tadpoles. First, they hatch underwater. Tadpoles have no legs or lungs. Instead, they use gills to breathe in the water. As they get older, they grow legs and lungs. Finally, they can live on land.

Every day, these tadpoles change. Even though they hatched in water, later they will live on land.

This eastern tiger salamander lives in Florida. It grew legs and lungs as it got older.

Salamanders are also amphibians. They look like lizards. However, they are not. Lizards are reptiles. They have dry, scaly skin. Salamanders have moist skin and no scales. They hatch from eggs in water. When they are young, they breathe in the water. At that stage, they have no legs. As they age, they grow legs. They also grow lungs so they can breathe on land.

Fast Fact

What happens if a salamander loses a leg or tail? No worries for the salamander—it grows back! Most vertebrates cannot grow new pieces of their body.

SEQUENCE **Explain how a frog changes as it grows.**

Fantastic Fish

You have probably seen fish in the wild. You may even have fish as pets. A **fish** is a vertebrate. It has a backbone. It spends its whole life in water. Instead of lungs, fish have gills.

Fish have scales. Their eggs hatch in water, like the eggs of amphibians. However, fish never leave the water. Fish take in oxygen from the water through gills. Since they do not have lungs, they cannot breathe in air. They would die on land.

There's a whole world under water! These fish breathe through gills. They live in shallow ocean water.

Great white sharks breathe through gills. Their great sense of smell and 3,000 sharp teeth make them fearsome hunters!

Most fish lay eggs and often don't wait for their eggs to hatch. Young fish must find their own way. Some fish will guard their eggs. Some male fish actually protect eggs by holding them in their mouths!

The great white shark is a fish that does not lay eggs. A female great white shark has live young. They swim away as soon as they are born and are on their on.

Fish do not need arms and legs. Instead, they have fins. Fins help them live in their watery world. Fins make swimming much easier.

COMPARE AND CONTRAST **How are fish like reptiles? How are they like amphibians?**

Different Worlds

From plants to vertebrates, all living things can grow, breathe, and reproduce. Living things also have traits that help them survive.

You have learned about the special traits of vertebrates. Mammals use their fur or hair to stay warm. Birds have wings and feathers to help them fly. Reptiles can live on land, but many also have webbed feet for swimming. Amphibians have gills when they hatch in water. They grow lungs and legs to help them make the move to land. Fish have gills and fins so they can live under water.

Focus Skill **CAUSE AND EFFECT** **How does growing lungs affect amphibians?**

This polar bear doesn't mind cold weather. Its furry coat helps keep it warm.

A lion is a mammal. That means it is covered in fur and gives live birth.

Summary

Vertebrates are animals with a backbone. There are five kinds of vertebrates. Mammals have fur or hair. They give birth to live young and make milk to feed them. Birds lay eggs. They have feathers instead of fur. Most reptiles also lay eggs. They have dry, scaly skin. Amphibians are born in water but grow up to have legs and lungs. Fish do not. Fish stay in water their entire lives. They take in oxygen through gills and swim using fins. The world is full of exciting vertebrates—including you!

Glossary

amphibian (am•FIB•ee•uhn) A type of vertebrate that has moist skin—and legs as an adult (10, 11, 12, 13, 14, 15)

bird (BERD) A type of vertebrate that has feathers (6, 7, 8, 9, 14, 15)

fish (FISH) A type of vertebrate that breathes through gills and spends its life in water (12, 13, 14, 15)

mammal (MAM•uhl) A type of vertebrate that has hair or fur and gives birth to live young (4, 5, 6, 7, 8, 9, 14, 15)

reptile (REP•tyl) A type of vertebrate that has dry skin covered with scales (8, 9, 10, 11, 13, 14, 15)

vertebrate (VER•tuh•brit) An animal with a backbone (2, 3, 4, 6, 8, 10, 11, 12, 14, 15)